understanding
# mental health

# ANXIETY and PHOBIAS

D1091984

## CARRIE IORIZZO

Crabtree Publishing Company
www.crabtreebooks.com

understanding mental health

**Developed and produced by Plan B Book Packagers**
www.planbbookpackagers.com
**Author:** Carrie Iorizzo
**Editorial director:** Ellen Rodger
**Art director:** Rosie Gowsell-Pattison
**Project coordinator:** Kathy Middleton
**Editor:** Molly Aloian
**Proofreader:** Wendy Scavuzzo
**Production coordinator and prepress
    technician:** Tammy McGarr
**Print coordinator:** Margaret Amy Salter

**Photographs:**
Cover, p. 1: Apollo Foto/Shutterstock.com;
p. 4: Kuzma/Shutterstock.com; p. 5: @erics/
Shutterstock.com; p. 6: Ilike/Shutterstock.com; p. 7:
Lasse Kristensen/Shutterstock.com; p. 8: Mopic/
Shutterstock.com; p. 9: Cobalt 88/Shutterstock.com;
p. 10: Platslee/Shutterstock.com; p. 11: Yuriy Rudyy/
Shutterstock.com; p. 12: Mopic/Shutterstock.com;
p. 14: Dwori/Shutterstock.com; p. 16: Sukiyaki/
Shutterstock.com; p. 17: Michiel de Wit/
Shutterstock.com; p. 18: Aleshyn Andrei/
Shutterstock.com; p. 19: Ioannis Pantzi/
Shutterstock.com; p. 20: Mopic/Shutterstock.com;
p. 22: Piotr Marcinski/Shutterstock.com; p. 23:
Stuart Jenner/Shutterstock.com; p. 25: Pressmaster/
Shutterstock.com; p. 26: Runzelkorn/Shutterstock.com;
p. 28: Franck Boston/Shutterstock.com; p. 29: O Driscoll
Imaging/Shutterstock.com; p.30: Peter Close/
Shutterstock.com; p. 32: Samuel Borges Photography/
Shutterstock.com; p. 34: Ollyy/Shutterstock.com; p. 35:
Razihusin/Shutterstock.com; p. 36: Vasilyev Alexandr/
Shutterstock.com; p. 37: Mast3r/Shutterstock.com; p.
38: Andrey Pavlov/Shutterstock.com; p. 39: Monkey
Business Images/Shutterstock.com; p. 40: Michael
Jung/Shutterstock.com; p. 42: Michael Jung/
Shutterstock.com; p. 43: Dan Kosmayer/
Shutterstock.com; p. 44: Picture Partners/
Shutterstock.com.

**Library and Archives Canada Cataloguing in Publication**

Iorizzo, Carrie, author
    Anxiety and phobias / Carrie Iorizzo.

(Understanding mental health)
Includes index.
Issued in print and electronic formats.
ISBN 978-0-7787-0082-1 (bound).--ISBN 978-0-7787-0088-3
(pbk.).--ISBN 978-1-4271-9395-7 (pdf).--ISBN 978-1-4271-9389-6
(html)


        1. Anxiety disorders--Juvenile literature.  2. Phobias--
Juvenile literature.  I. Title.

RC531.I67 2013        j616.85'22        C2013-906484-2
                                        C2013-906485-0

**Library of Congress Cataloging-in-Publication Data**

Iorizzo, Carrie, author.
   Anxiety and phobias / Carrie Iorizzo.
      pages cm. -- (Understanding mental health)
   Audience: 10-13.
   Audience: Grade 7 to 8.
   Includes index.
   ISBN 978-0-7787-0082-1 (reinforced library binding : alk. paper)
-- ISBN 978-0-7787-0088-3 (pbk. : alk. paper) -- ISBN 978-1-4271-
9395-7 (electronic pdf : alk. paper) -- ISBN 978-1-4271-9389-6
(electronic html : alk. paper)
   1. Anxiety--Juvenile literature. 2.  Phobias--Juvenile literature.
3.  Obsessive-compulsive disorder--Juvenile literature.  I. Title.

RC535.I57 2014
616.85'22--dc23
                                        2013037007

# Crabtree Publishing Company
www.crabtreebooks.com        1-800-387-7650

Printed in Canada/102013/BF20130920

**Published in Canada**
**Crabtree Publishing**
616 Welland Ave.
St. Catharines, ON
L2M 5V6

**Published in the United States**
**Crabtree Publishing**
PMB 59051
350 Fifth Avenue, 59th Floor
New York, New York 10118

**Published in the United Kingdom**
**Crabtree Publishing**
Maritime House
Basin Road North, Hove
BN41 1WR

**Published in Australia**
**Crabtree Publishing**
3 Charles Street
Coburg North
VIC, 3058

# CONTENTS

Totally Freaked                     5

What Is Anxiety?                    9

What Are Phobias?                  17

Diagnosis and Treatment           21

Dealing With Stigma               29

Managing Fear                     35

Friends and Family                39

Coping Toolbox                    42

Other Resources                   46

Glossary & Index                  48

Anxiety disorders are mental health disorders, or illnesses that are treatable. Anxiety is the body's natural response to danger or perceived danger. Sometimes people have too much anxiety and it interferes with normal living.

# Totally Freaked

"I think I've been like this—anxious—my entire life.
Even when I was a little kid, I used to get these awful stomachaches.
Or in the morning, I'd get a headache and my mom would let me stay home
from school. I was always worried. I worried about what I was wearing,
if people liked me or not, and how I was going to do on a test. I also worried
about my mom dying, or war breaking out, or bugs in my food, or getting a
disease and being sick. Sometimes I couldn't sleep at all
and there would be so many thoughts in my head.

One day, the school called my mom because I totally
freaked out and couldn't stop crying. I hadn't
slept for three days. She decided I had
to see a doctor. My doctor told me I had
a condition called anxiety that could
be made better."

— Hannah, 15

# Let's Talk About Mental Health

Talking about mental health and mental illness is not easy. People with mental health issues, or illnesses such as anxiety disorders, have often been shunned or attacked. Mental illness has traditionally not been well accepted by society. People with a mental illness have been called crazy, stupid, lazy, and weak. They have been wrongly associated with violence, bizarre behavior, and criminal activity. These associations are called **stigmas** because they shame people for having a mental health disorder. Stigmas are based on a lack of understanding and a fear of mental illness.

# Stigma and Shame

The stigma, or shame, of being mentally ill often keeps people from getting the help they need to recover. Stigma can lead to feelings of decreased self-worth and can make the symptoms of the illness worse. A person with a mental illness often feels that the negative comments people make about them are true. Sometimes the stigma is so overwhelming that the person may even think about suicide. As people become more informed about mental illness, they become more aware of the how to deal with stigma and stereotypes.

Shame should not be a part of any illness. Often, fighting stigma means fighting ignorance.

## What Is Mental Illness?

We know a lot about the brain and how it works, but there is still so much we don't know. It is the most complicated organ in your body. What researchers do know is that even the smallest change in the chemistry of your brain can cause serious health problems. Changes in the make-up and functioning of your gray matter can cause disease. Some of these diseases are mild and can be treated easily. Others are more serious and may need a lifetime of medical attention, much like other medical conditions and diseases such as diabetes or heart disease. Some mental illnesses can be severe enough to cause disability, while others are easy to manage. Often, mental health problems can be treated with medication and therapy such as counseling.

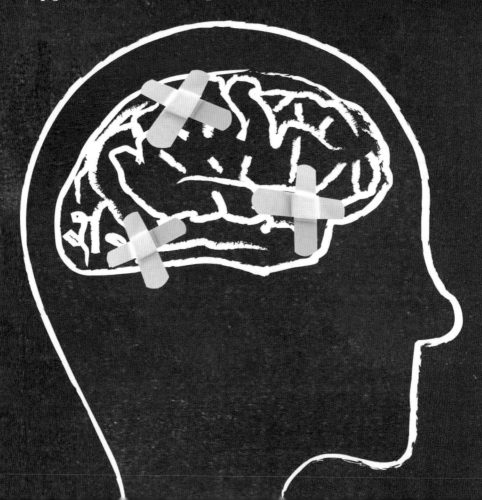

Sometimes anxiety can make it feel like you are in a giant maze and can't find your way out.

# What Is Anxiety?

*chapter 1*

Anxiety is the fear and uncertainty you feel when you're under pressure or stress. It's a natural and normal response that is a little like the feelings you have when you are in a play. When the worry is severe, just won't go away, and interferes with your daily living, you might have an anxiety disorder.

Anxiety disorder is a term used by doctors and **psychologists** to explain several **psychiatric disorders** that involve excessive worrying and fear about real or imagined situations. These intense feelings of anxiety can get worse if not treated. But they usually have no grounding in what is actually happening or about to happen. That does not make them feel any less real. Often, a person with an anxiety disorder knows there is no reason to worry. But they just can't stop. Badgering them, making fun of them, or yelling at them, does not make the feelings disappear. Often, it only makes them worse. To be diagnosed with anxiety by a doctor, you need to be anxious and fearful continuously over a period of six months or more.

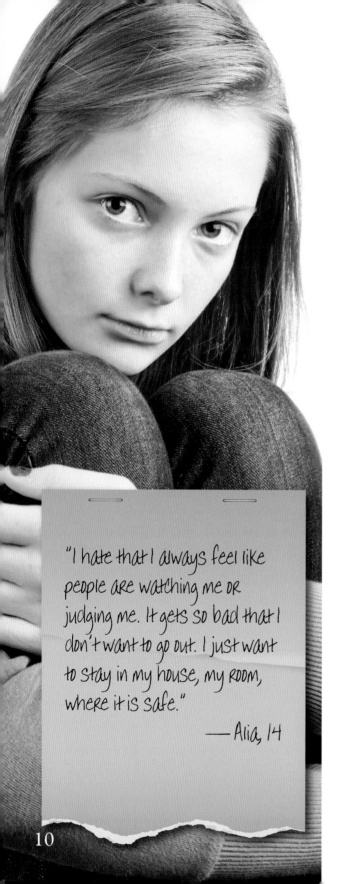

"I hate that I always feel like people are watching me or judging me. It gets so bad that I don't want to go out. I just want to stay in my house, my room, where it is safe."

—Alia, 14

## Body Signs

Signs and symptoms of anxiety disorders can vary from person to person. They are different than the normal feelings of anxiousness you might feel before a big game or when you have to speak in front of the class. Anxiety disorders are marked by intense and overwhelming emotions of fear and panic. You may experience recurring nightmares or thoughts and memories that just won't go away. You may feel sick to your stomach or have bowel problems. You might even vomit. Your heart may start to pound, or you may get butterflies in your stomach, or headaches, tense muscles, or even shortness of breath. You may be unable to sleep or stay asleep. Fear and anxiety can make you break out in a sweat and feel light-headed or dizzy. Feelings of being out of control or crazy are also common with anxiety disorders.

## What Causes Anxiety?

Anxiety is a normal response to real danger. Everybody has anxiety from time to time. It helps people adapt to stressful situations such as writing a test or avoiding an accident. An anxiety disorder is when our bodies react to danger when there is no danger. Brain research is an expanding field. Some new research has found that the areas of the brain that help people overcome fear is less active in people with anxiety disorders. Other research has shown that some people may have been exposed to **trauma** as children that would make them more likely to be anxious. Some researchers also feel that there is a **genetic** connection to anxiety and that having someone in the family with an anxiety disorder can also make you more likely to have one yourself.

It can be hard to get to sleep or stay asleep with so many anxious thoughts in your head.

# Types of Anxiety

There are several different types of anxiety disorders, each with their own specific symptoms. All of these disorders have one thing in common, they are all rooted in overwhelming fear that is often **irrational**. They include:

- **Generalized anxiety disorder (GAD)**: GAD is the constant worrying about, well...everything. People with GAD can become so worried that they are unable to perform the tasks of daily living. Their worry can become paralyzing. GAD usually starts out slowly in teens and becomes more prominent over time.

- **Panic disorder**: Panic disorders affect over six million Americans. They are aptly named. An "attack" can occur at any time, including during sleep. Panic attacks feel overwhelming. Your heart pounds, you may be short of breath, have chest pain, and you may feel smothered. You may even think you are having a heart attack. There is an overpowering sense of doom along with nausea, chills, and sweating. A panic attack peaks in about ten minutes and then begins to subside.

- **Post traumatic stress disorder (PTSD)**: PTSD is an anxiety disorder that usually occurs when someone has experienced a traumatic, and often life-threatening event such as a car crash, war, or physical or sexual abuse. Long after the event has passed, through flashbacks, people with PTSD still feel as though they are reliving the event.

- **Phobias**: Phobias are ongoing fears of a thing, such as snakes, or a situation, such as the fear of using a public washroom, that are pronounced and distressing for the person suffering from the phobia.

- **Obsessive-compulsive disorder (OCD)**: People who have OCD have persistent thoughts, ideas, or images in their heads that often compel them to act in repetitive ways. They may feel the need to check and recheck things before they can move on to their daily living. Doing things repeatedly is an attempt to stop the persistent thoughts or obsessions.

- **Social anxiety disorder**: People with social anxiety disorder are afraid of what other people say and think about them. They are terrified that they are being judged. This anxiety may prevent them from going to school and being around friends. For some, social anxiety only occurs during certain events. For others, it happens whenever they are around people.

Anxiety may seem enormous, but nothing is too big to treat.

## Wait...There's More

People who have anxiety disorders sometimes have other mental health issues. In medical terms, this is called comorbidity. Comorbidity is a technical (and slightly scary sounding) word that means that there are two diseases happening at once.

It means people with anxiety may also suffer from depression, phobias, or panic attacks. Using alcohol or drugs in an attempt to remain calm or bolster self-confidence is also common with anxiety disorders. Substance use can lead to substance abuse when people need to repeatedly use alcohol or drugs to get through a situation that makes them anxious.

Some people with anxiety disorders use alcohol or drugs to quiet the symptoms, but this just makes them worse.

## Can't Stop the Thoughts

One out of eight young people has symptoms of anxiety. Many people with anxiety disorders understand that their feelings of fear are irrational, or not always based on fact, but they can't stop them. They have sleepless nights, are afraid, and often insecure. Some people's grades suffer because they spend a lot of time feeling, fighting, and hiding their anxiety. They may also feel ashamed that they cannot control their thoughts and this can contribute to self-esteem problems. The important thing to know is that anxiety can be treated and its symptoms diminish with treatment.

## You're Not Alone

A lot of people struggle with anxiety disorders. Some suffer silently and try to hide or ignore how they feel. Ignoring anxiety or avoiding situations that produce anxiety does not mean the condition will magically disappear. In fact, not dealing with anxiety can make it worse. You can only push your anxious feelings down for so long before they come bubbling up again.

## Quick Facts on Anxiety

Of all the people who suffer from a mental health disorder or illness, it is estimated that only one in ten seek treatment. This is sad, because mental illness is, like many other illnesses, treatable.

- Researchers believe that common mental disorders in adults first emerge in childhood and adolescence.

- Anxiety disorders are comprised of a number of disorders. Together they form the most common mental illness.

- While all ages between 13 and 18 seem to suffer from anxiety disorder at about the same rate, there is a difference between girls and boys. Girls are more likely to have anxiety disorders than boys. For males, about 20 percent will become ill with an anxiety disorder, compared to 30 percent of females.

According to the National Institute for Mental Health, about 8 percent of teens aged 13-18 have an anxiety disorder, but only 18 percent of those get help.

A dog can be perfectly harmless, but to a person with a dog phobia, or cynophobia, just being near a dog will create feelings of fear and panic.

# Chapter 2

# What Are Phobias?

Phobias are excessive and irrational fears of a thing or a situation. A friend who is afraid of dogs, who believes all dogs attack humans, and will do anything to get away from them, likely has a dog phobia. If you have an unreasonable fear of crowds, think you are going to be harmed in a crowd, and cannot go to gatherings with more than a few people without feeling dizzy, sweaty, or sick, you may have a crowd phobia.

People who have a phobia have an overwhelming and paralyzing fear of objects, animals, situations, and things. They may not understand that the fear is unfounded. Phobias have identifiable **triggers** that set off the fearfulness. Many phobias happen when people are exposed to a fearful situation. But people who are phobic can get anxious and fearful just by thinking about a thing, an object, or a situation.

Snakes will make most people jump, but Ophidiophobia is an irrational fear of snakes and what they might do.

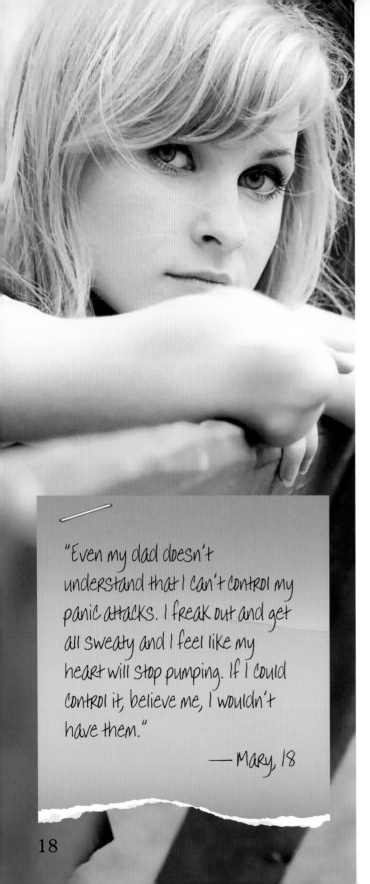

"Even my dad doesn't understand that I can't control my panic attacks. I freak out and get all sweaty and I feel like my heart will stop pumping. If I could control it, believe me, I wouldn't have them."

— Mary, 18

## Subtypes

Psychologists believe phobias are **subtypes** of anxiety disorders. This means they are a specific kind, or category of anxiety. There are three main types of phobias: general social phobia, specific social phobia, and agoraphobia. General social phobia is also called social anxiety. Specific social phobia is fear and anxiety triggered by a specific situation such as speaking in a crowd, or a thing such as spiders, dogs, or heights. Agoraphobia is a fear of leaving a "safe space" such as home.

There are hundreds of different phobias, and many ways to be agoraphobic. Just simply naming a phobia does not begin to describe how a person experiences their phobia. Phobias can be mild. They can also be very severe and life altering.

## How Does It Feel?

An agoraphobic person might fear leaving home because the outside world is too large and uncontrolled. They may also fear touching things outside their home because they believe them to be **contaminated**. Traveling outdoors, even for short distances, can cause their heart to race. They can feel sick to their stomach, sweaty, and like they are going to pass out. They may believe they are going to die if they are outside of their safe places.

Phobias produce real and frightening symptoms.

## Anxiety Disorders vs. Phobias

What's the difference between having an anxiety disorder and having a phobia? Both illnesses stem from an ungrounded fear or terror that lasts for months or, in some cases, for years. Phobias tend to have their origins in things that happened during childhood. People with phobias tend to avoid situations or things that trigger their phobias. However, if they become exposed to what causes their fear, a type of anxiety, known as a panic attack, usually occurs. The good news is that with treatment and therapy, it is possible to control phobia symptoms and live a life without unreasonable fear.

Diagnosis and treatment are the first steps to a life without overwhelming fear. They are a way out of the darkness.

# Chapter 3

# Diagnosis and Treatment

Your adolescent and teen years are the years to set personal goals for the rest of your life. It's a time to get to know yourself and what you want out of life. It's also a time to kick up your heels and enjoy yourself before your working years begin. However, anxiety can slowly destroy this wonderful time in your life.

## It's Real

Having anxiety is no different than having a physical illness. If you were diagnosed with diabetes you would expect to watch your diet and be on medication for your entire life. But that doesn't mean you can't have a full and exciting life. It just means you have to take care of yourself, see your doctor regularly, and take your medications. It's the same with anxiety disorders. The first step is recognizing that you need professional help. Professional help means visiting your doctor or a **psychiatrist** to be diagnosed. You can also see a psychologist or counselor to understand your anxiety. They can help you see how your specific disorder affects you and your behavior.

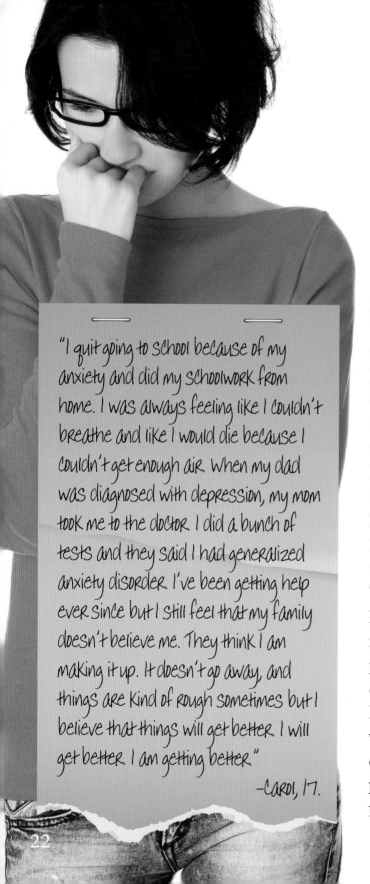

"I quit going to school because of my anxiety and did my schoolwork from home. I was always feeling like I couldn't breathe and like I would die because I couldn't get enough air. When my dad was diagnosed with depression, my mom took me to the doctor. I did a bunch of tests and they said I had generalized anxiety disorder. I've been getting help ever since but I still feel that my family doesn't believe me. They think I am making it up. It doesn't go away, and things are kind of rough sometimes but I believe that things will get better. I will get better. I am getting better."

—Carol, 17.

## Seeking Help

It's hard knowing you are struggling with something but not knowing what it is and how to get help. Seeking help through a doctor or a counselor is a good place to start. The sooner you get your mental health disorder diagnosed, the sooner you can begin treatment and feel better. If you don't know who to approach, try asking someone you trust such as a teacher or school counselor. If they can't or won't help, don't give up. Try a helpline. They are often listed online and you can contact them anonymously. The operators are trained to help. It's important to remember that anxiety and phobias do not just go away. They can get worse. But the good news is that with the proper diagnosis, and medical and psychological treatment, you can lead a normal life.

## Talking About It

There are many physical ailments and complications that can go hand-in-hand with anxiety disorders. When you see your doctor, he or she will ask you questions to help diagnose your condition. He or she may interview you and ask you to rate your symptoms. Your doctor will want to rule out any major physical problems. He or she may order tests to make sure you are physically okay. The doctor will ask for some personal information about you and your family. Talk about any substance abuse problems, family issues, strange thoughts, and weird feelings. Tell your doctor everything. Don't be shy. Your mental health and physical well-being depends on it. Remember that a doctor-patient relationship is **confidential**, and any information you give is between you and your doctor.

If your doctor or counselor dismisses your symptoms or feelings, find a new one who will listen.

# What Does Treatment Involve?

Once you are diagnosed with an anxiety disorder, there are a number of effective treatments available. It may take some time for you, your doctor, and psychologist to figure out what works best for your specific anxiety disorder and symptoms. Often, medication is used to treat **debilitating** symptoms, and therapy is used to help you change and understand your behavior. Here are some common treatments:

- **Medication** — Numerous types of medications are available to help relieve anxiety disorders. These are prescribed by your doctor or a psychiatrist.

- **Cognitive-Behavioral Therapy** — CBT is a talk therapy that helps you find the feelings and thoughts that cause your anxiety. Once the causes are found, you learn new and healthier ways to cope with the anxiety.

- **Managing Stress** — There are many useful stress reduction techniques available such as breathing exercises, **visualization**, meditation, yoga, and massage. Studies show exercise is very useful for alleviating anxiety symptoms.

- **Counseling** — One-on-one discussions with a therapist, such as a psychologist, can help you talk through your feelings and situation. Being open with a therapist can be a little frightening at first and may even trigger anxiety or a panic attack. The therapist is not there to judge or criticize you. He or she will help you understand what you are going through and that you are normal and your illness is real and treatable. Therapy sessions are usually confidential depending on your age. Your therapist will go over the ground rules at your first appointment.

- **Programs and Group Work** —Various programs exist that offer therapy sessions through community mental health associations, clinics, schools, and sometimes in camps and other relaxing areas. Day programs are often run by clinics or in group sessions while you live at home. Many offer programs that involve the entire family to improve relationships at home and help your family members understand mental health.

Exercise can help you deal with stress and anxiety because it has been proven to alter brain chemistry.

## Coping With a Diagnosis

Anxiety disorders are the most common psychiatric disorders diagnosed in children and teens. That doesn't mean they are easy to diagnose. Often, anxiety is brushed off as "just a phase" or something an individual should be able to control on their own. But that's missing the point. Ignoring symptoms or believing you can will them away does not fix or get rid of a person's anxiety. A diagnosis is an acknowledgment that an anxiety disorder exists and is persistent, or long term. Once you have a diagnosis, you can begin to move on and get help, including counseling or medication that tackle the triggers and the symptoms.

Using alcohol or drugs to cope with a mental health disorder is called self-medicating. It's always a bad idea because it can lead to complications and addiction.

# Drug Therapy

Medications play an important role in managing the symptoms of anxiety disorders and phobias. They alter the chemical environment in your brain to help you maintain an ongoing calm and relaxed state. Doctors often advise using medication with other therapies such as counseling and cognitive behavioral therapy (CBT). Studies have shown that CBT and drug therapy worked better in children aged 7 to 17 than just drug therapy or CBT alone.

Anti-depressant drugs called selective serotonin reuptake inhibitors (SSRIs) are often prescribed to teens with severe anxiety disorders. These drugs, such as fluoxetine and paroxetine, influence the brain chemicals called neurotransmitters. Neurotransmitters allow brain cells to communicate with each other, like telephone wires. Anti-depressants assist in correcting imbalances with these chemicals. Some SSRIs can increase suicidal thoughts and behaviors in some adolescents and teenagers. It is important to know all the facts about a drug before taking it. Anti-depressants should be taken on a regular basis and should only be stopped under a doctor's supervision. Stopping these drugs can cause you to feel depressed and possibly suicidal. They should also not be taken with alcohol.

Some drugs are prescribed to be taken just in case of a sudden attack, and for a limited time, similar to using an asthma inhaler. They are called benzodiazepines and they are prescribed less often to young people because they can be addictive.

It isn't easy being "different" and it can be worse when stigma makes a person feel ashamed of themselves.

# Chapter 4
# Dealing With Stigma

You are probably familiar with the term "stigma." Anxiety disorders, like all mental health issues, carry a stigma. Stigma is an invisible shame or mark of disgrace that many people who have a mental illness must deal with. They don't ask to be judged because of their mental health. They just are. Stigma is a negative attitude or **prejudiced** beliefs about mental illness. Stigma includes bullying, excluding, abusing, or punishing people. If you believe that people who have a snake phobia are just weak-minded and stupid, you are perpetuating, or keeping alive, a stigma.

People feel uncomfortable talking about mental health. It isn't viewed like other health issues such as cancer. Many people don't understand mental illness, or they think that people can choose how they behave.

The stigma of a mental health disorder can make the symptoms worse because they put pressure on a person to "act normal" so they won't be ridiculed.

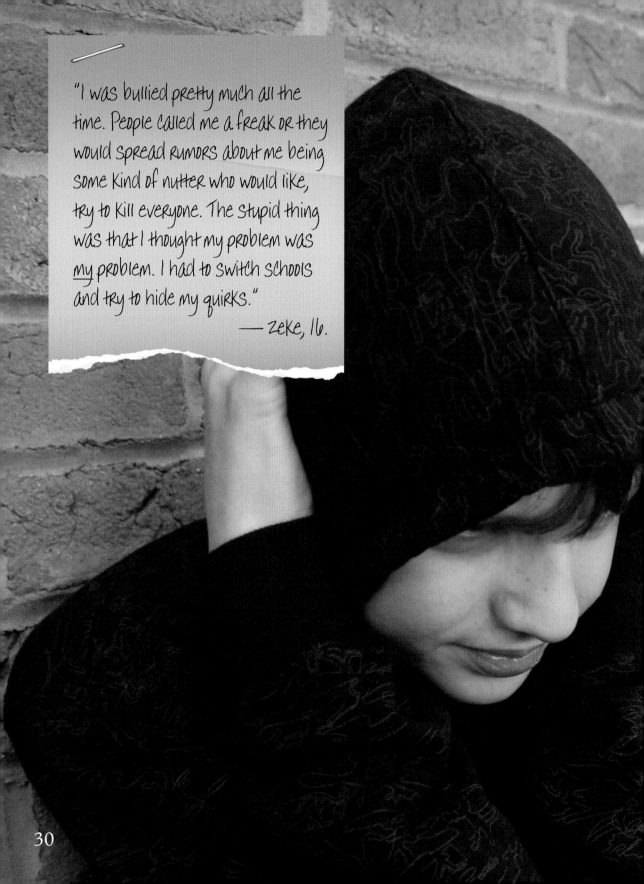

"I was bullied pretty much all the time. People called me a freak or they would spread rumors about me being some kind of nutter who would like, try to kill everyone. The stupid thing was that I thought my problem was my problem. I had to switch schools and try to hide my quirks."

— Zeke, 16.

# Awareness

Society as a whole has a poor understanding of mental health. Even families who have a member in their household with an anxiety disorder sometimes refuse to acknowledge the illness. Instead they may ignore the obvious and believe there is nothing to be done. People with anxiety disorders are often labeled as lazy, or undisciplined—sometimes even when the disorder is acknowledged. This stigma and lack of knowledge about mental health can keep people from seeking help, or if they have been diagnosed, it keeps them from continuing with their meds and therapy.

# Mental Health Misperceptions

Misperceptions of what mental illness is and isn't cause a lot of heartache and pain. Anxiety disorders and phobias are illnesses, the same as any physical ailment. And like any other type of disease, people with anxiety disorders don't want to feel this way. They want to be well. Some people turn to drugs and alcohol to self-medicate in hopes that will make things better. Others who are diagnosed and in treatment will stop taking their medications and attending therapy because of shame. They don't want to feel different or depressed or be treated like an outcast.

# Discrimination and Hate

Discrimination and prejudice keep almost two-thirds of all people with a mental health problem from getting help. Many are afraid of being rejected by their family and friends. They are often stereotyped. How would you feel if someone called you crazy or "mental"? People with mental health disorders deal with this daily. With an anxiety disorder, this additional pressure can add to the fear of being judged.

# Understanding Mental Illness

Mental illnesses can affect anyone of any race, age, **income**, or religion. They affect how a person thinks, acts, feels, and deals with other people. It can affect their daily living, their moods, and their ability to cope. The thing with mental illness is that people who have a disorder do not look different. Their eyes don't turn red and they don't grow a toaster from their head. It is a silent and invisible illness. Often, the only way you will know if someone has a mental health problem is if they tell you. And if they tell you, you should feel honored because it means they trust you. If they trust you, you need to respect them and not react with fear or revulsion. You could also ask if they need help and how you can help. Having trusted people who support you is a key part of good mental health.

People with anxiety disorders may look happy and carefree, but they are trying to fit in and not be labeled as different or difficult.

# How You Can Stop the Stigma

One way to stop the stigma surrounding mental illness is to be informed. It's important to know myth from fact when it comes to mental health. It's also important to know that your attitude and actions can make a difference in people's lives. Here is a list to help you learn how to stop the stigma:

1. Be aware that young people, including children, are affected by mental health problems. Experts believe up to 70 percent of adult mental illness begins during childhood or adolescence. People don't make up their mental health problems.

2. Mental health disorders often have many causes but the main ones, like all diseases, are biological and environmental. A person who has a mental health disorder is not "at fault." Neither they nor their parents caused the illness.

3. An anxiety disorder is not a character flaw or a sign of a weak mind.

4. What you say and how you act are important. Calling people names, spreading gossip, or being otherwise hurtful is just plain mean. Just like other **slurs**, calling people crazy or nuts is inappropriate, nasty, and rude.

5. Treat people with a mental health problem the way you would like to be treated. Support your classmates, friends, or family members.

6. Educate yourself and keep a positive attitude. If you find people spreading myths, give them the facts.

34

# Chapter 5

# Managing Fear

When you have an anxiety disorder, managing your fear can feel like a full-time job. This is especially true if you don't have anyone to talk to about your fears. Many people feel better if they have a professional who can help them manage their condition. A professional can be a psychiatrist, doctor, psychologist, or social worker. A medical or psychological professional will help give you the information and confidence you need to manage your anxiety in all sorts of situations.

Managing fear begins with being prepared. You can be prepared by setting up a crisis plan. A crisis plan is a guide that outlines some things to do when your anxiety is especially hard to handle. It is important to realize that when you are stressed or out of sorts, you may rely on your "fight or flight" behavior. Doing a crisis plan ahead of time will help you focus and remind you that you won't always feel the way you do when you are super anxious, or in crisis.

Without a crisis plan, things can blow up out of proportion.

# Make a Crisis Plan

A crisis plan should remind you of how you have felt when you were really anxious or panicked before and how you managed to feel better. It is a process that involves asking yourself questions, answering them, and getting to know yourself and how you behave. Make and keep a copy of your plan. If you feel comfortable, ask someone you trust to keep a copy for you. Here are some sample questions:

1. What situations, people, or things make you anxious?

2. Why do they make you anxious? Make a list.

3. How do you feel when you are anxious or close to a panic attack?

4. How do you act in these situations? Are you aware?

5. What things, actions, or thoughts have helped you during an anxious period in the past? What things have not helped?

6. Who can help you when you are feeling anxious and stressed? Make a list.

7. Do you have a safety plan if you are experiencing a severe anxiety or panic attack in a place outside of your home?

# Trigger Finger

Triggers are things that bring on negative or obsessive thoughts and anxiety. Everyone has different triggers and it is important to know your own. Figure out what your triggers are and how you can minimize them. Here are some suggestions to help manage your triggers:

1. Avoid negative self-talk. Change the way you talk to yourself.

2. Avoid getting overtired. Too little sleep and too little exercise can make anxiety worse.

3. Talk about your feelings. Do not hold them in.

4. Do not put too much pressure on yourself.

5. Practice deep breathing.

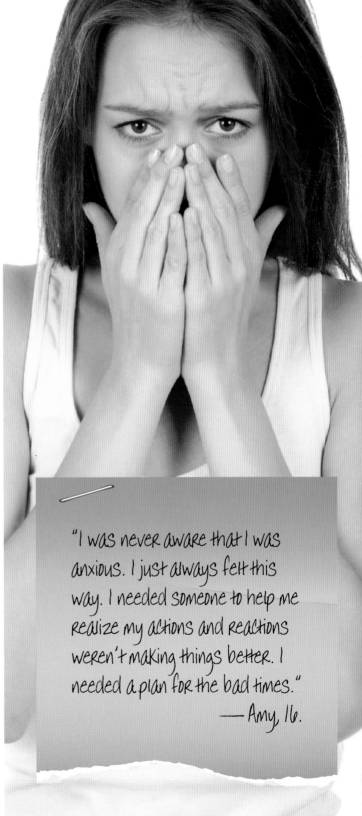

"I was never aware that I was anxious. I just always felt this way. I needed someone to help me realize my actions and reactions weren't making things better. I needed a plan for the bad times."
— Amy, 16.

Dealing with a mental health issue
is a team effort.

# chapter 6

# Friends and Family

Living with someone who has an anxiety disorder or phobia can be challenging. You may feel frustrated, angry, and embarrassed. You may not understand what they are going through and how their disease affects how they act. Sometimes their behavior may seem irrational and confusing. It's normal for you and the rest of your family to be stressed and sometimes feel helpless.

Spending time together and talking is one way to help a loved one.

## Dealing with Guilt

You love your parent or sibling. But there are days when you might feel like leaving and never coming back. Or you might wish that they were not a part of your family. It's important to know that you're not alone and there are things that you can do to help yourself and your loved one. Understanding the ins and outs of phobias and anxiety disorders can help you prepare for any situations that may arise. Being there for your loved one, supporting them, and getting them help when needed can help them feel less stressed. If they are undiagnosed, encourage them to see a doctor, or offer to go with them. Let them know you care about their health.

## Being There

It is exhausting to be constantly supportive and patient. Sometimes you will need your mental and physical strength to take care of yourself too. This means not always focusing on the needs of the person with the illness. You need to take time out to do things that you enjoy.

Feeling guilty about taking time for yourself is only natural. It can help if you have someone—a friend, a trusted relative, teacher, or counselor—to talk to about your feelings. Some mental health organizations have sibling and caregiver groups that meet and offer support and advice to family and friends.

"I never realized my dad's problem was anxiety. We just lived with his drinking (because of his anxiety) and ignored things. It was really bad because he was miserable and I hated him for so long for that. Years later, with treatment, he became a different person. If only that could have happened when I was a kid."

— Sarah, 21.

# Caregiver Support Checklist

Caregivers, or carers, are usually relatives or friends who provide support to children or adults with a mental illness. Support means many things. It could mean a sibling who looks after a younger or older child. It could mean a youth who cooks, cleans, or ensures an adult takes their meds. The constant demands of caregiving make it a tough job. Caregivers can often feel overwhelmed by many things, including a loved one's diagnosis and the responsibilities they may take on because of it. Children with a parent who has an anxiety disorder may not want to burden their parents by sharing their own fears about the future. Here are some suggestions for understanding your feelings:

1. Know that you cannot always "fix" things or make things better. You are not responsible for the illness.

2. Mental illness isn't a one-way trip. A person can feel better for a while and then feel worse. Not everyone accepts their diagnosis or wants to make the changes to feel better, such as attending doctor's appointments or taking meds.

3. Feeling resentful, guilty, frustrated, or angry is normal. So is feeling embarrassed by a parent or sibling's behavior. It is important to talk to someone about your feelings.

4. You may feel fear that you too will develop the disorder. This is natural. Talking to a trusted adult about your concerns can help you feel better.

5. Take up a hobby or sport that is just for you. Exercise helps relieve stress and releases brain chemicals that make you feel better.

# Chapter 7

# Coping Toolbox

Putting together positive plans, or a coping toolbox, provides you with strategies on how to handle your more stressful moments. Your toolbox should contain a number of healthy options that you can use when anxiety is getting the best of you and you are too overwhelmed to think clearly.

## Assembly Required

Building your toolbox should be a positive experience. Do it when you are relaxed and calm. You can jot ideas down on a notepad or have an actual binder or box with individual pages for each coping strategy. If you can, start with at least five positive things to say or do when you are stressed. As you continue, keep adding different coping skills to the toolbox. Remember, this toolbox is unique to you. These strategies are what work for you. If you try one and it doesn't calm you, toss it and add another one that you think is more effective.

# Pack Your Box

Keep a journal to learn what triggers your anxiety and examine it for patterns. Make a plan for positivity and include in it actions such as meditation, visualization, and distraction exercises. Meditation provides a quiet space where you can calm yourself and get your head together. Visualization is a great way to work on positive thoughts. Distraction exercises can include anything from reading a book to listening to music.

- Make a list of positive affirmations or sayings that you can use, such as: "I am calm and relaxed," or "I am in complete control of my life and my situation at all times," or "I feel great!"

- Call your best friend. BFFs are a great way to boost a negative mood. Talk to him or her about how you're feeling. Try clearing your mind by reminiscing about something funny the two of you did.

- Take the dog for a walk. Ride a bike, go to the gym, or check out the mall. Exercise can give you a feeling of balance and make you feel relaxed.

- Practice deep breathing. In a quiet place, inhale slowly through your nose and exhale out your mouth. Pay attention to your breath and feel yourself relax.

- Don't try to be perfect. Don't take on too many tasks at once. Set small and reachable goals.

## Stop the Top

Often, people with an anxiety disorder describe how they cannot shut their brains off. When they are overly anxious, they feel like a spinning top. "Thought spinning" is continuous and persistent thinking. It's sort of like a song you can't get out of your head. These racing thoughts are usually negative and self-defeating. They feel like they have no end and can cause a lot of stress. Avoiding this type of thinking is easier than you might think. Next time you feel yourself getting caught up in a neverending spiral, stop for a moment and take some slow, deep breaths to help refocus your attention on something else. Don't be so hard on yourself. If a friend was going through the same thing, would you criticize them or would you give them a break? Face the fear. Fear is only an emotion. Let it wash over you. In your mind, walk around it, make fun of it. See it for what it is—an **illusion**.

Stop the spinning with positive behaviors.

# Self-Care 101

When anxiety overwhelms you, treat yourself with care and concern. Keep your thoughts kind and supportive. Develop a self-care routine to keep your anxiety in check. Here are some techniques to help overcome overpowering emotions:

- When you feel yourself becoming anxious, take a moment to analyze how you feel. If you can't do it during the episode, do it immediately after.

- Keep a journal so you can track what exactly you do during the anxious moments. Are you overeating, at school, in class, drinking alcohol, or taking drugs?

- Once you know what causes the anxiety, expose yourself to it in a controlled environment. Plan how you will handle it. Face at least one of your triggers each day. Show yourself that your strength is greater than the anxiety.

- Keep a journal and write down your thoughts, fears, and worries. Keep track of the challenges you faced during the day and how you handled them.

- Positive Thinking – Keeping negative thoughts out of your mind requires practice. Begin by taking notice every time a negative or anxious thought enters your mind. Replace it with a positive thought. For enforcement, wear an elastic band around your wrist and snap it when you repeat a positive thought.

# Other Resources

There is reliable information on anxiety disorders and phobias, but you have to know where to look. Check your school or local library for books. You can also check the internet for websites and hotlines. Be careful when searching websites. Not every site gives trustworthy or factual information. Here are some good resources to start with:

## Helpful Hotlines
### National Alliance on Mental Illness
### 1-800-950-6264
This is a toll free (U.S.) 10 a.m. to 6 p.m. (EST) national hotline staffed with trained volunteers who can supply information and support for anyone (adolescents, teens, friends, parents) with questions about mental illness.

### National Suicide Hotline
### 1-800-SUICIDE (784-2433)
This toll-free 24-hour national service connects you to a trained counselor at a nearby suicide crisis center. The service is confidential.

### Kids Help Phone
### 1-800-668-6868
A free, confidential, 24-hour hotline staffed by professional counselors. Supports youths who are in crisis and need help and information on a number of issues. Hotline available in Canada only. Visit their website at www.kidshelpphone.ca

# Websites

## National Alliance on Mental Illness
## www.nami.org

This site provides trusted information on mental illnesses such as anxiety disorders, as well as treatment information and where to find support and help. Content is available in English and Spanish.

## Anxiety and Depression Association of America
## www.adaa.org

A site with trusted facts on anxiety disorders including how to get help. A section on anxiety and depression in children and teens provides personal stories of managing anxiety and thriving with the disorder.

## Mind Your Mind
## mindyourmind.ca

An informational teen-oriented mental health site with information on how to get help as well as personal stories about coping, struggles, and successes, a blog, and interactive tools that can help you identify and cope with your mental health disorder.

## Teens Health
## kidshealth.org

A safe information source on all aspects of teen health, including mental health. Available in English or Spanish.

## Teen Mental Health
## teenmentalhealth.org

A useful website on a number of mental health topics for youths, their families, and teachers. The site focuses on evidence-based medicine, with trustworthy research articles.

# Glossary

**confidential** Something kept secret or private

**contaminated** Something made unpure by exposure to a polluting substance

**debilitating** To make very ill and unable to function normally

**genetic** Something relating to genes that is inherited or passed on from a parent or other relative

**illusion** A false belief, or seeing something that isn't there

**income** Money received through work, or how much money a person has per year

**irrational** Something that is not logical or reasonable

**prejudiced** A preconceived opinion of dislike or distrust

**psychiatric disorders** Mental illnesses

**psychiatrist** A medical doctor who specializes in treating mental illness

**psychologist** Someone who is trained, and often licensed, to treat people with psychological disorders

**slurs** Insulting, hurtful, or rude remarks and allegations made against a person

**stigma** Shame associated with a particular illness or behavior

**trauma** Emotional shock that follows a stressful event or experience that can lead to long-term emotional pain or distress

**visualization** To form a mental image of something, or imagining or picturing something in your head

# Index

agoraphobia 18, 19
brain 7, 26
causes 11
cognitive behavioral therapy 24, 27
comorbidity 14
counseling 7, 21–27
crisis plan 35–37
diagnosis 21–23, 26
family 11, 22, 23, 25, 31, 33, 39–41

fear management 35–37, 42–45
generalized anxiety disorder 12, 22
genetic connection 11
medications 7, 21, 24, 26, 27, 31
obsessive compulsive disorder 13, 37
panic 10, 12, 14, 18, 19, 24, 36

phobias 12, 14, 17–19, 22, 27, 29, 31, 39
post traumatic stress disorder 12
psychiatrists 21, 24, 35
psychologists 9, 18, 21, 24, 35
self-medicating 26, 31

social anxiety disorder 13, 18
social phobias 18–19
stigma 6, 29–33
symptoms 6, 10, 12–13, 14, 19, 24, 26, 27, 29
toolbox 42–45
treatment 24–27
triggers 17, 18, 19, 24, 26, 37, 43, 45